50 Creative Hot Dog Recipes

By: Kelly Johnson

Table of Contents

- Chili Cheese Dog
- Korean BBQ Hot Dog
- Buffalo Chicken Dog
- Mac and Cheese Dog
- Taco Dog
- BBQ Pulled Pork Dog
- Mediterranean Hot Dog with Feta and Tzatziki
- Breakfast Dog with Eggs and Bacon
- Sloppy Joe Dog
- Reuben Dog
- Pineapple Teriyaki Dog
- Caprese Hot Dog with Mozzarella and Basil
- Jalapeño Popper Dog
- Mediterranean Lamb Dog
- Philly Cheesesteak Hot Dog
- Sweet and Spicy Mango Dog
- Vegan Beet Dog
- Chicago-Style Hot Dog
- Coney Island Hot Dog
- Maple Bacon Dog
- Pesto and Sun-Dried Tomato Dog
- Lobster Roll Hot Dog
- Spicy Sriracha Dog
- Banh Mi Hot Dog
- Grilled Veggie Dog
- Garlic Parmesan Hot Dog
- Kimchi Dog
- Currywurst Hot Dog
- Spinach and Feta Dog
- Hawaiian Hot Dog with Grilled Pineapple
- Loaded Nacho Dog
- Shrimp Po' Boy Hot Dog
- Cranberry BBQ Hot Dog
- Italian Sausage Dog with Peppers
- Sweet Potato and Black Bean Dog
- BBQ Chicken and Coleslaw Dog

- Eggplant Parmesan Dog
- Fried Pickle Dog
- Truffle and Mushroom Dog
- Clam Chowder Dog
- Thai Peanut Sauce Dog
- Pumpkin Spice Hot Dog
- Spicy Crab Dog
- Italian Meatball Dog
- Bourbon Bacon Jam Dog
- Veggie Sautéed Dog
- Fried Mac and Cheese Dog
- Citrus Shrimp Dog
- Cherry Cola BBQ Dog
- Moroccan-Spiced Hot Dog

Chili Cheese Dog

Ingredients:

- 4 hot dog sausages
- 4 hot dog buns
- 1 cup chili (homemade or canned)
- 1 cup shredded cheddar cheese
- Chopped green onions for garnish

Instructions:

1. Cook the hot dogs according to package instructions (grill, boil, or pan-fry).
2. Toast the buns lightly if desired.
3. Place each hot dog in a bun and top with chili.
4. Sprinkle shredded cheddar cheese on top and garnish with chopped green onions.

Korean BBQ Hot Dog

Ingredients:

- 4 hot dog sausages
- 4 hot dog buns
- 1/2 cup Korean BBQ sauce
- 1/4 cup kimchi, chopped
- Sliced green onions for garnish

Instructions:

1. Cook the hot dogs according to package instructions.
2. Toast the buns lightly if desired.
3. Drizzle Korean BBQ sauce over each hot dog.
4. Top with kimchi and sliced green onions before serving.

Buffalo Chicken Dog

Ingredients:

- 4 hot dog sausages
- 4 hot dog buns
- 1 cup shredded cooked chicken
- 1/4 cup buffalo sauce
- 1/2 cup ranch dressing
- Chopped celery for garnish

Instructions:

1. Cook the hot dogs according to package instructions.
2. In a bowl, mix shredded chicken with buffalo sauce.
3. Toast the buns lightly if desired.
4. Place a hot dog in each bun and top with buffalo chicken mixture.
5. Drizzle ranch dressing and garnish with chopped celery.

Mac and Cheese Dog

Ingredients:

- 4 hot dog sausages
- 4 hot dog buns
- 1 cup macaroni and cheese (homemade or store-bought)
- Crumbled bacon for garnish (optional)

Instructions:

1. Cook the hot dogs according to package instructions.
2. Toast the buns lightly if desired.
3. Place each hot dog in a bun and top with macaroni and cheese.
4. Sprinkle crumbled bacon on top if using.

Taco Dog

Ingredients:

- 4 hot dog sausages
- 4 hot dog buns
- 1 cup cooked ground beef or turkey
- 1/2 cup taco sauce
- Shredded lettuce, diced tomatoes, and cheese for toppings

Instructions:

1. Cook the hot dogs according to package instructions.
2. Toast the buns lightly if desired.
3. Place each hot dog in a bun and top with cooked ground meat and taco sauce.
4. Add shredded lettuce, diced tomatoes, and cheese as desired.

BBQ Pulled Pork Dog

Ingredients:

- 4 hot dog sausages
- 4 hot dog buns
- 1 cup pulled pork (cooked and sauced)
- Coleslaw for topping

Instructions:

1. Cook the hot dogs according to package instructions.
2. Toast the buns lightly if desired.
3. Place each hot dog in a bun and top with pulled pork.
4. Add coleslaw on top before serving.

Mediterranean Hot Dog with Feta and Tzatziki

Ingredients:

- 4 hot dog sausages
- 4 hot dog buns
- 1/2 cup tzatziki sauce
- 1/2 cup feta cheese, crumbled
- Chopped cucumbers and olives for garnish

Instructions:

1. Cook the hot dogs according to package instructions.
2. Toast the buns lightly if desired.
3. Spread tzatziki sauce on each bun and place a hot dog inside.
4. Top with crumbled feta, chopped cucumbers, and olives.

Breakfast Dog with Eggs and Bacon

Ingredients:

- 4 hot dog sausages
- 4 hot dog buns
- 4 scrambled eggs
- 4 slices cooked bacon, crumbled
- Shredded cheese for topping

Instructions:

1. Cook the hot dogs according to package instructions.
2. Toast the buns lightly if desired.
3. Place each hot dog in a bun and top with scrambled eggs.
4. Sprinkle crumbled bacon and shredded cheese on top before serving.

Sloppy Joe Dog

Ingredients:

- 4 hot dog sausages
- 4 hot dog buns
- 1 cup sloppy joe mixture (homemade or canned)
- Shredded cheddar cheese for topping
- Pickles for garnish

Instructions:

1. Cook the hot dogs according to package instructions.
2. Toast the buns lightly if desired.
3. Place each hot dog in a bun and top with sloppy joe mixture.
4. Sprinkle shredded cheddar cheese on top and garnish with pickles.

Reuben Dog

Ingredients:

- 4 hot dog sausages
- 4 hot dog buns
- 1 cup sauerkraut, drained
- 1/2 cup corned beef, chopped
- 1/4 cup thousand island dressing
- Swiss cheese slices

Instructions:

1. Cook the hot dogs according to package instructions.
2. Toast the buns lightly if desired.
3. Place each hot dog in a bun and top with chopped corned beef and sauerkraut.
4. Drizzle with thousand island dressing and top with a slice of Swiss cheese.

Pineapple Teriyaki Dog

Ingredients:

- 4 hot dog sausages
- 4 hot dog buns
- 1/2 cup teriyaki sauce
- 1/2 cup grilled pineapple, chopped
- Sliced green onions for garnish

Instructions:

1. Cook the hot dogs according to package instructions.
2. Toast the buns lightly if desired.
3. Brush each hot dog with teriyaki sauce.
4. Top with grilled pineapple and garnish with sliced green onions.

Caprese Hot Dog with Mozzarella and Basil

Ingredients:

- 4 hot dog sausages
- 4 hot dog buns
- 1/2 cup fresh mozzarella balls, halved
- 1/2 cup cherry tomatoes, halved
- Fresh basil leaves
- Balsamic glaze for drizzling

Instructions:

1. Cook the hot dogs according to package instructions.
2. Toast the buns lightly if desired.
3. Place each hot dog in a bun and top with mozzarella and cherry tomatoes.
4. Add fresh basil leaves and drizzle with balsamic glaze.

Jalapeño Popper Dog

Ingredients:

- 4 hot dog sausages
- 4 hot dog buns
- 1/2 cup cream cheese, softened
- 1/2 cup jalapeños, diced (fresh or pickled)
- Crumbled bacon for topping
- Shredded cheese for topping

Instructions:

1. Cook the hot dogs according to package instructions.
2. Toast the buns lightly if desired.
3. Spread cream cheese on each bun and place a hot dog inside.
4. Top with diced jalapeños, crumbled bacon, and shredded cheese.

Mediterranean Lamb Dog

Ingredients:

- 4 hot dog sausages (lamb or beef)
- 4 hot dog buns
- 1/2 cup tzatziki sauce
- 1/2 cup chopped cucumbers
- Crumbled feta cheese for topping
- Fresh mint leaves for garnish

Instructions:

1. Cook the hot dogs according to package instructions.
2. Toast the buns lightly if desired.
3. Spread tzatziki sauce on each bun and place a hot dog inside.
4. Top with chopped cucumbers, crumbled feta, and fresh mint leaves.

Philly Cheesesteak Hot Dog

Ingredients:

- 4 hot dog sausages
- 4 hot dog buns
- 1 cup cooked and chopped steak
- 1/2 cup sautéed bell peppers and onions
- Provolone cheese slices

Instructions:

1. Cook the hot dogs according to package instructions.
2. Toast the buns lightly if desired.
3. Place each hot dog in a bun and top with chopped steak and sautéed veggies.
4. Add a slice of provolone cheese on top and melt under a broiler if desired.

Sweet and Spicy Mango Dog

Ingredients:

- 4 hot dog sausages
- 4 hot dog buns
- 1/2 cup mango salsa (diced mango, onion, cilantro, lime juice)
- 1 tbsp sriracha sauce (optional)
- Fresh cilantro for garnish

Instructions:

1. Cook the hot dogs according to package instructions.
2. Toast the buns lightly if desired.
3. Place each hot dog in a bun and top with mango salsa.
4. Drizzle with sriracha if using and garnish with fresh cilantro.

Vegan Beet Dog

Ingredients:

- 4 large beets, peeled and cut into hot dog shapes
- 4 hot dog buns
- 1/4 cup vegan mayo
- 1 tbsp Dijon mustard
- Shredded lettuce
- Diced tomatoes for topping

Instructions:

1. Roast the beet "hot dogs" in the oven at 400°F (200°C) for about 30-40 minutes until tender.
2. Toast the buns lightly if desired.
3. Spread vegan mayo and Dijon mustard on each bun.
4. Place a beet dog in each bun and top with shredded lettuce and diced tomatoes.

Chicago-Style Hot Dog

Ingredients:

- 4 hot dog sausages
- 4 poppy seed buns
- Yellow mustard
- Chopped onions
- Sweet green pickle relish
- Tomato slices
- Pickled sport peppers
- Celery salt

Instructions:

1. Cook the hot dogs according to package instructions.
2. Place each hot dog in a poppy seed bun.
3. Add yellow mustard, chopped onions, relish, tomato slices, and sport peppers on top.
4. Sprinkle with celery salt before serving.

Coney Island Hot Dog

Ingredients:

- 4 hot dog sausages
- 4 hot dog buns
- 1 cup chili (homemade or canned)
- Chopped onions
- Shredded cheddar cheese for topping

Instructions:

1. Cook the hot dogs according to package instructions.
2. Toast the buns lightly if desired.
3. Place each hot dog in a bun and top with hot chili.
4. Sprinkle with chopped onions and shredded cheddar cheese.

Maple Bacon Dog

Ingredients:

- 4 hot dog sausages
- 4 hot dog buns
- 4 slices of cooked bacon
- 1/4 cup maple syrup
- Chopped green onions for garnish

Instructions:

1. Cook the hot dogs according to package instructions.
2. Toast the buns lightly if desired.
3. Place each hot dog in a bun and wrap with a slice of bacon.
4. Drizzle with maple syrup and garnish with chopped green onions.

Pesto and Sun-Dried Tomato Dog

Ingredients:

- 4 hot dog sausages
- 4 hot dog buns
- 1/4 cup pesto
- 1/4 cup sun-dried tomatoes, chopped
- Arugula for topping

Instructions:

1. Cook the hot dogs according to package instructions.
2. Toast the buns lightly if desired.
3. Spread pesto on each bun and place a hot dog inside.
4. Top with chopped sun-dried tomatoes and arugula.

Lobster Roll Hot Dog

Ingredients:

- 4 hot dog sausages (or lobster sausage)
- 4 hot dog buns
- 1 cup cooked lobster meat, chopped
- 1/4 cup mayonnaise
- 1 tbsp lemon juice
- Chopped chives for garnish

Instructions:

1. Cook the hot dogs according to package instructions.
2. Toast the buns lightly if desired.
3. In a bowl, mix chopped lobster with mayonnaise and lemon juice.
4. Place each hot dog in a bun and top with lobster mixture.
5. Garnish with chopped chives.

Spicy Sriracha Dog

Ingredients:

- 4 hot dog sausages
- 4 hot dog buns
- 1/4 cup mayonnaise
- 2 tbsp sriracha sauce
- Sliced jalapeños for topping
- Cilantro for garnish

Instructions:

1. Cook the hot dogs according to package instructions.
2. Toast the buns lightly if desired.
3. In a small bowl, mix mayonnaise with sriracha sauce.
4. Spread the spicy mayo on each bun, place a hot dog inside, and top with sliced jalapeños and cilantro.

Banh Mi Hot Dog

Ingredients:

- 4 hot dog sausages
- 4 baguette-style hot dog buns
- Pickled carrots and daikon (carrots and daikon radish pickled in vinegar)
- Cucumber slices
- Fresh cilantro
- Sriracha mayo (mayonnaise mixed with sriracha)

Instructions:

1. Cook the hot dogs according to package instructions.
2. Toast the buns lightly if desired.
3. Spread sriracha mayo on each bun.
4. Place each hot dog in a bun and top with pickled carrots, daikon, cucumber slices, and fresh cilantro.

Grilled Veggie Dog

Ingredients:

- 4 veggie hot dogs
- 4 whole wheat buns
- 1 zucchini, sliced
- 1 bell pepper, sliced
- Olive oil
- Salt and pepper
- Mustard or your favorite sauce for topping

Instructions:

1. Preheat the grill to medium heat.
2. Toss the zucchini and bell pepper slices in olive oil, salt, and pepper.
3. Grill the veggie hot dogs and vegetable slices for about 5-7 minutes, turning occasionally.
4. Serve the hot dogs in buns and top with grilled vegetables and mustard or sauce.

Garlic Parmesan Hot Dog

Ingredients:

- 4 hot dog sausages
- 4 hot dog buns
- 1/4 cup butter, melted
- 3 cloves garlic, minced
- 1/2 cup grated Parmesan cheese
- Fresh parsley, chopped for garnish

Instructions:

1. Cook the hot dogs according to package instructions.
2. In a bowl, mix melted butter and minced garlic.
3. Brush the garlic butter on each bun and sprinkle with Parmesan cheese.
4. Toast the buns on the grill until golden.
5. Place the hot dogs inside and garnish with chopped parsley.

Kimchi Dog

Ingredients:

- 4 hot dog sausages
- 4 hot dog buns
- 1 cup kimchi, chopped
- 1/4 cup mayonnaise
- 1 tsp sriracha (optional)

Instructions:

1. Cook the hot dogs according to package instructions.
2. Toast the buns lightly if desired.
3. In a bowl, mix mayonnaise with sriracha (if using).
4. Spread the spicy mayo on each bun, place a hot dog inside, and top with chopped kimchi.

Currywurst Hot Dog

Ingredients:

- 4 hot dog sausages
- 4 hot dog buns
- 1 cup ketchup
- 2 tbsp curry powder
- Chopped onions for topping

Instructions:

1. Cook the hot dogs according to package instructions.
2. In a small saucepan, mix ketchup with curry powder and heat through.
3. Toast the buns lightly if desired.
4. Place each hot dog in a bun and top with the curry ketchup and chopped onions.

Spinach and Feta Dog

Ingredients:

- 4 hot dog sausages
- 4 hot dog buns
- 1 cup fresh spinach, sautéed
- 1/2 cup crumbled feta cheese
- Tzatziki sauce for topping

Instructions:

1. Cook the hot dogs according to package instructions.
2. Sauté fresh spinach until wilted.
3. Toast the buns lightly if desired.
4. Place each hot dog in a bun and top with sautéed spinach, crumbled feta, and tzatziki sauce.

Hawaiian Hot Dog with Grilled Pineapple

Ingredients:

- 4 hot dog sausages
- 4 hot dog buns
- 1 cup fresh pineapple, sliced
- Teriyaki sauce for drizzling
- Green onions, chopped for garnish

Instructions:

1. Preheat the grill to medium heat.
2. Grill the hot dogs and pineapple slices for about 3-4 minutes until grill marks appear.
3. Toast the buns lightly if desired.
4. Place each hot dog in a bun, top with grilled pineapple, drizzle with teriyaki sauce, and garnish with chopped green onions.

Loaded Nacho Dog

Ingredients:

- 4 hot dog sausages
- 4 hot dog buns
- 1 cup tortilla chips, crushed
- 1 cup nacho cheese sauce
- Jalapeños, sliced for topping
- Sour cream for drizzling

Instructions:

1. Cook the hot dogs according to package instructions.
2. Toast the buns lightly if desired.
3. Place each hot dog in a bun and top with crushed tortilla chips, nacho cheese sauce, jalapeños, and a drizzle of sour cream.

Shrimp Po' Boy Hot Dog

Ingredients:

- 4 hot dog sausages
- 4 hot dog buns
- 1 cup cooked shrimp, chopped
- 1/4 cup remoulade sauce
- Shredded lettuce
- Sliced tomatoes

Instructions:

1. Cook the hot dogs according to package instructions.
2. Toast the buns lightly if desired.
3. In a bowl, mix chopped shrimp with remoulade sauce.
4. Place each hot dog in a bun, top with shrimp mixture, shredded lettuce, and sliced tomatoes.

Cranberry BBQ Hot Dog

Ingredients:

- 4 hot dog sausages
- 4 hot dog buns
- 1 cup cranberry sauce
- 1/2 cup BBQ sauce
- Fresh parsley for garnish

Instructions:

1. Cook the hot dogs according to package instructions.
2. In a bowl, mix cranberry sauce and BBQ sauce until combined.
3. Toast the buns lightly if desired.
4. Place each hot dog in a bun and top with the cranberry BBQ sauce. Garnish with fresh parsley.

Italian Sausage Dog with Peppers

Ingredients:

- 4 Italian sausage links
- 4 hoagie rolls
- 1 red bell pepper, sliced
- 1 green bell pepper, sliced
- 1 onion, sliced
- Olive oil
- Italian seasoning

Instructions:

1. Preheat the grill to medium heat.
2. In a skillet, sauté the peppers and onion in olive oil with Italian seasoning until tender.
3. Grill the Italian sausages until cooked through.
4. Toast the hoagie rolls lightly if desired.
5. Place each sausage in a roll and top with sautéed peppers and onions.

Sweet Potato and Black Bean Dog

Ingredients:

- 4 veggie hot dogs
- 4 whole wheat buns
- 1 cup sweet potato, roasted and mashed
- 1 cup black beans, drained and rinsed
- Avocado, sliced for topping

Instructions:

1. Cook the veggie hot dogs according to package instructions.
2. Roast sweet potatoes until soft, then mash.
3. Toast the buns lightly if desired.
4. Place each hot dog in a bun and top with mashed sweet potato, black beans, and avocado slices.

BBQ Chicken and Coleslaw Dog

Ingredients:

- 4 hot dog sausages
- 4 hot dog buns
- 1 cup cooked chicken, shredded
- 1/2 cup BBQ sauce
- 1 cup coleslaw

Instructions:

1. Cook the hot dogs according to package instructions.
2. Mix shredded chicken with BBQ sauce until well coated.
3. Toast the buns lightly if desired.
4. Place each hot dog in a bun, top with BBQ chicken, and finish with coleslaw.

Eggplant Parmesan Dog

Ingredients:

- 4 hot dog sausages
- 4 hot dog buns
- 1 eggplant, sliced and breaded
- Marinara sauce
- Mozzarella cheese, shredded
- Fresh basil for garnish

Instructions:

1. Preheat the oven to 375°F (190°C).
2. Bread and bake the eggplant slices until golden and crispy.
3. Cook the hot dogs according to package instructions.
4. Toast the buns lightly if desired.
5. Place each hot dog in a bun, top with baked eggplant, marinara sauce, and mozzarella cheese. Garnish with fresh basil.

Fried Pickle Dog

Ingredients:

- 4 hot dog sausages
- 4 hot dog buns
- 1 cup dill pickle slices, breaded and fried
- Ranch dressing for drizzling

Instructions:

1. Cook the hot dogs according to package instructions.
2. Bread and fry dill pickle slices until crispy.
3. Toast the buns lightly if desired.
4. Place each hot dog in a bun, top with fried pickles, and drizzle with ranch dressing.

Truffle and Mushroom Dog

Ingredients:

- 4 hot dog sausages
- 4 hot dog buns
- 1 cup mushrooms, sautéed
- 2 tbsp truffle oil
- Fresh arugula for topping

Instructions:

1. Cook the hot dogs according to package instructions.
2. Sauté mushrooms until golden, then toss with truffle oil.
3. Toast the buns lightly if desired.
4. Place each hot dog in a bun, top with sautéed mushrooms, and finish with fresh arugula.

Clam Chowder Dog

Ingredients:

- 4 hot dog sausages
- 4 hot dog buns
- 1 cup clam chowder (prepared)
- Chopped chives for garnish

Instructions:

1. Cook the hot dogs according to package instructions.
2. Heat clam chowder in a saucepan until warm.
3. Toast the buns lightly if desired.
4. Place each hot dog in a bun and ladle clam chowder over the top. Garnish with chopped chives.

Thai Peanut Sauce Dog

Ingredients:

- 4 hot dog sausages
- 4 hot dog buns
- 1/2 cup Thai peanut sauce
- Shredded carrots for topping
- Chopped peanuts for garnish
- Fresh cilantro for garnish

Instructions:

1. Cook the hot dogs according to package instructions.
2. Toast the buns lightly if desired.
3. Place each hot dog in a bun and drizzle with Thai peanut sauce.
4. Top with shredded carrots, chopped peanuts, and fresh cilantro.

Pumpkin Spice Hot Dog

Ingredients:

- 4 hot dog sausages
- 4 hot dog buns
- 1 cup pumpkin puree
- 1 tsp pumpkin pie spice
- 1/4 cup cream cheese, softened
- 1/4 cup maple syrup

Instructions:

1. Cook the hot dogs according to package instructions.
2. In a bowl, mix pumpkin puree, pumpkin pie spice, cream cheese, and maple syrup until smooth.
3. Toast the buns lightly if desired.
4. Place each hot dog in a bun and top with the pumpkin mixture.

Spicy Crab Dog

Ingredients:

- 4 hot dog sausages
- 4 hot dog buns
- 1 cup crab meat, shredded
- 2 tbsp mayonnaise
- 1 tbsp sriracha
- Chopped green onions for garnish

Instructions:

1. Cook the hot dogs according to package instructions.
2. In a bowl, mix crab meat, mayonnaise, and sriracha until well combined.
3. Toast the buns lightly if desired.
4. Place each hot dog in a bun and top with the spicy crab mixture. Garnish with chopped green onions.

Italian Meatball Dog

Ingredients:

- 4 hot dog sausages
- 4 hoagie rolls
- 1 cup cooked meatballs, sliced
- 1 cup marinara sauce
- Mozzarella cheese, shredded
- Fresh basil for garnish

Instructions:

1. Preheat the oven to 375°F (190°C).
2. Cook the hot dogs according to package instructions.
3. In a saucepan, heat marinara sauce and add sliced meatballs until warmed.
4. Toast the hoagie rolls lightly if desired.
5. Place each sausage in a roll, top with meatballs, marinara sauce, and mozzarella cheese. Bake until cheese is melted. Garnish with fresh basil.

Bourbon Bacon Jam Dog

Ingredients:

- 4 hot dog sausages
- 4 hot dog buns
- 1 cup bacon, cooked and crumbled
- 1/2 cup bourbon whiskey
- 1/4 cup brown sugar
- 1/4 cup diced onions

Instructions:

1. Cook the hot dogs according to package instructions.
2. In a skillet, cook diced onions until soft, then add bacon, bourbon, and brown sugar. Cook until thickened.
3. Toast the buns lightly if desired.
4. Place each hot dog in a bun and top with the bourbon bacon jam.

Veggie Sautéed Dog

Ingredients:

- 4 hot dog sausages
- 4 hot dog buns
- 1 cup mixed vegetables (bell peppers, onions, zucchini), sautéed
- Olive oil
- Italian seasoning

Instructions:

1. Cook the hot dogs according to package instructions.
2. In a skillet, sauté mixed vegetables in olive oil with Italian seasoning until tender.
3. Toast the buns lightly if desired.
4. Place each hot dog in a bun and top with sautéed vegetables.

Fried Mac and Cheese Dog

Ingredients:

- 4 hot dog sausages
- 4 hot dog buns
- 1 cup mac and cheese (prepared)
- 1 cup breadcrumbs
- Oil for frying

Instructions:

1. Cook the hot dogs according to package instructions.
2. Prepare mac and cheese and let it cool. Form into small balls and coat with breadcrumbs.
3. Fry the mac and cheese balls until golden brown.
4. Toast the buns lightly if desired.
5. Place each hot dog in a bun, top with fried mac and cheese balls.

Citrus Shrimp Dog

Ingredients:

- 4 hot dog sausages
- 4 hot dog buns
- 1 cup shrimp, cooked and chopped
- Zest and juice of 1 lime
- Chopped cilantro for garnish
- Avocado slices for topping

Instructions:

1. Cook the hot dogs according to package instructions.
2. In a bowl, mix chopped shrimp with lime zest and juice.
3. Toast the buns lightly if desired.
4. Place each hot dog in a bun and top with citrus shrimp mixture, avocado slices, and cilantro.

Cherry Cola BBQ Dog

Ingredients:

- 4 hot dog sausages
- 4 hot dog buns
- 1 cup cherry cola
- 1/2 cup BBQ sauce
- Sliced pickles for topping
- Chopped green onions for garnish

Instructions:

1. In a saucepan, combine cherry cola and BBQ sauce over medium heat. Simmer until slightly thickened.
2. Cook the hot dogs according to package instructions.
3. Toast the buns lightly if desired.
4. Place each hot dog in a bun and drizzle with cherry cola BBQ sauce. Top with sliced pickles and garnish with chopped green onions.

Moroccan-Spiced Hot Dog

Ingredients:

- 4 hot dog sausages
- 4 pita bread or hot dog buns
- 1/2 cup hummus
- 1 tsp ground cumin
- 1 tsp ground coriander
- 1/2 tsp cinnamon
- Chopped fresh mint for garnish
- Diced cucumbers and tomatoes for topping

Instructions:

1. Cook the hot dogs according to package instructions.
2. In a small bowl, mix hummus with cumin, coriander, and cinnamon.
3. Toast the pita bread or buns lightly if desired.
4. Place each hot dog in a pita or bun, spread the spiced hummus on top, and add diced cucumbers and tomatoes. Garnish with fresh mint.